Nights
TO IMAGINE

Magical

Places to Stay

in America

BY PETER GUTTMAN

Fodor's Travel Publications, Inc.

New York • Toronto • London • Sydney • Auckland

HTTP://WWW.FODORS.COM/

Copyright © 1996 by Peter Guttman

Fodor's is a registered trademark of Fodor's Travel Publications, Inc.

ISBN 0-679-03341-6
First Edition

Library of Congress Cataloging-in-Publication Data
Guttman, Peter, 1954–
   Nights to imagine: magical places to stay
   in America / by Peter Guttman.
      p. cm.
   ISBN 0-679-03341-6 (alk. paper)
   1. Hotels—United States—Guidebooks.
   I. Title.
TX907.2.G88 1996
647.9473'01—dc20   96-19568
                    CIP

Special Sales
Fodor's Travel Publications are available at special discounts for bulk purchases for sales promotions or premiums. Special editions, including personalized covers, excerpts of existing guides, and corporate imprints, can be created in large quantities for special needs. For more information, contact your local bookseller or Special Markets, Fodor's Travel Publications, 201 E. 50th Street, New York, NY 10022. Inquiries from Canada should be directed to your local Canadian bookseller or sent to Random House of Canada, Ltd., Marketing Dept., 1265 Aerowood Drive, Mississauga, Ontario L4W 1B9. Inquiries from the United Kingdom should be sent to Fodor's Travel Publications, 20 Vauxhall Bridge Road, London, England SW1V 2SA.

Acknowledgments
Forever thanks to Lori Greene for her amazing grace. With deep appreciation for Fabrizio La Rocca's exquisite patience and guidance.

Credits
Fabrizio La Rocca, Editor and Creative Director
Candice Gianetti, Text Editor
Allison Saltzman, Designer
Jolie Novak, Editorial Assistant

PRINTED IN CHINA
10 9 8 7 6 5 4 3 2 1

Lovingly dedicated to my mom, Judith, whose spirit and humor sparked my enthusiasm, and my dad, Arthur, whose wisdom and curiosity fired my imagination.

CONTENTS

Imagine playing a starring role in one of your favorite dreams—while you're wide awake. Usually dreams are a nocturnal activity, a necessary escape valve allowing us to safely go a little insane each evening. But living them out can be a powerful way to push the boundaries of daily existence, and travel—a physical leap into the unknown—provides a perfect opportunity to do just that.

Traveling through life, I always seem to tote around a ragged suitcase stuffed with dreams and carefully measured doses of insanity. That may be how I came to awaken one morning to a suboceanic bedside staring competition with an unblinking barracuda. It explains how spending time behind iron bars became a desirable, if temporary, lifestyle choice. It's even why I started writing this in a swaying shed high in the branches of an oak tree. The colorful

adventures I try to cram into life— birthdays, anniversaries, holidays toasted on battleships, in fire lookout towers, underwater and overjoyed—are a reassuring yardstick of my days spent on planet Earth. For me, genuine travel requires a blend of wonder and curiosity. It's not just about seeing foreign lands, but seeing the foreign in familiar territory. Even though I've slipped through messy penguin rookeries in Antarctica and clambered across vine-rope bridges to attend tribal pig roasts in Papua New Guinea, the spray of dirt kicked up on cattle drives through the Rockies or the foghorn that announces a craggy Atlantic coastline still sets my adrenaline pumping.

Within the nooks and crannies of the American landscape, an abundance of serendipitous discoveries awaits, gift-wrapped by the asphalt ribbon that detours off the beaten path. Never fond of sitting in the bumper-to-bumper monotony of the routine world, I find it more rewarding to watch the crowds dissolve into specks in my rear-view mirror. I tend to bypass the freeway's cookie-cutter pit stops, motel chains, and fast-food franchises to seek the exit ramp that separates the traveler from the tourist. In my years poking around America's dusty byways, I've managed to harvest a healthy crop of lodgings that defy mediocrity. Some are remote outposts in fragile cahoots with nature. Others, perhaps right around the corner, present the bedroom as theatrical experience or create their own quirky universe in the midst of a busy city. All are vibrant expressions of the American character, of our distinctive pioneer heritage and the entrepreneurial spirit it engendered.

This treasury of magical bedtime stories is a celebration of fantasy, a carefully hand-picked selection of getaways that either whisper romance, scream eccentricity, or burst at the seams with the promise of adventure. Whichever you choose, I hope they sharpen your appetite for the smorgasbord of life. For dreamers, satisfaction is virtually guaranteed. You'll know it in those few fleeting moments at the margins of consciousness when, as your weary head melts into the pillow in some strange and unforgettable new place, you find yourself longing for just a few more nights to imagine.

Peter Guttman
New York, 1996

Isle au Haut, Maine

Keeper's House

At the fishing village of Stonington, near where the sun first shines in America, hop aboard a mailboat and head out to sea toward Isle au Haut, a speck of granite on the cusp of a continent. Anchored on a cliff is a snug outpost overlooking the crashing ocean and the sweeping crimson beam of a lighthouse. Built in 1907, the Keeper's House is a fiercely romantic place, still illuminated only by kerosene lanterns and furnished in dollhouse-cozy decor.

A day here passes lazily, with mushrooming in the ferny woods and exploring the mollusk-encrusted gardens of marine life unveiled at low tide. Before a candlelit dinner, linger awhile on the porch to spy through the telescope on hardworking lobstermen hauling their traps. As darkness falls, count the distant lighthouses that form a sparkling maritime necklace across the horizon. When thick mists roll over the spruce-clad headlands, drift toward slumber to the sound of a baritone foghorn.

Glen Canyon National Recreation Area, Arizona/Utah

Lake Powell
Houseboats

A vast stretch of tectonic dreamscape straddling the Arizona-Utah border, the Lake Powell wilderness is most fully experienced by houseboat, with ports of call tailored to your whim. The lake's glassy turquoise waters, guarded by towering jags of ancient sandstone, survey more than a thousand tortuous miles of gnarled buttes and mesas. Chauffeuring your own floating apartment through this geologic layer cake is a Huck Finn fantasy. Thread a slender nautical path through chasms that cleave steep vermilion cliffs, and encounter hidden box canyons or isolated sandy coves that tempt the anchor off the boat. Try one of the sage-scented hiking trails to find disintegrating ancient Anasazi ruins or solitary natural bridges sculpted by eons of erosion. In the evening, fish for walleye from the deck, barbecue your prizes at the edge of soaring rock amphitheaters, then sit back and enjoy the visual symphony of shooting stars and overcrowded constellations in the inky desert sky.

Lake Mohonk, New York

Mohonk Mountain

Deep in Rip Van Winkle country, a Bunyanesque castle stretches its hodge-podge of chalets, turrets, and chimneys over an eighth of a mile. Straddling a granite knife-edge that slices the shore of a canoe-spattered lake, the secluded Mohonk Mountain House is edged with wooden walkways and gazebos that perch falconlike atop glacial boulders. With 7,500 acres of wilderness for a backyard, the resort offers old-fashioned pleasures that seem torn from a Currier & Ives calendar. Autumn leaves shade horse-drawn surreys before the plunging thermometer creates scenes from a just-shaken snow globe. Hardy souls glide across the frozen lake on chair-skates pushed by chivalrous companions, then

House

warm before one of the inn's 250 fire-places. In spring, dormant hikers and climbers emerge to tackle the dramatic Shawangunk escarpments. On the Victorian porch in summer, guests ease into rocking chairs to enjoy the gardens and sip oceans of lemonade— a reminder of the teetotaling heritage of this serene Quaker enclave.

New Orleans, Louisiana

Delta Queen

Steaming along the Mississippi River past an antebellum landscape of plantation homes cradled by live oaks, the *Delta Queen* steers a course through America's heartland and another era. As hoop-skirted belles wave from the levee, the gingerbread-trimmed floating wedding cake is propelled through an obstacle course of hidden sandbars and shifting bends by a cherry red paddlewheel that whips the muddy river into a frothy spray. At the sternwheeler's heart is the engine room, a Rube Goldberg concoction of pulsing cylinders, throbbing pistons, clanking valves, and snorting blasts of heated vapor. At night, Jell-O–colored clouds of steam spewed from a calliope toss Stephen Foster tunes into the jasmine-kissed breeze. Live Dixieland wafts from the saloon, where a sarsaparilla helps wash down spicy Cajun shrimp étouffée. On this floating island of festive anachronisms, the atmospherics of card-playing riverboat gamblers, sing-alongs, and kite-flying contests allow you to inhabit the world of Mark Twain and adopt its gentle, lazy rhythms.

Forlornly anchored in stormy Aleutian waters, Round Island receives one of the world's largest migrations of walrus each year. While few humans can seize the rare opportunity to eavesdrop on an unruly bachelor party of 15,000 grunting, ivory-tusked pinnipeds,

Round Island, Alaska

Walrus Islands

State Game Sanctuary

those who do—equipped with a sleeping permit, a tent capable of withstanding hurricane-force winds, and enough food to outlast a long stranding—will find this wildflower-carpeted nugget of an island a rewarding haven. Negotiate precipitous trails past cliffside kittiwake rookeries to observe the whiskered men's club breaking their seasonal travels with a nap along the shore. In a comic ballet of insomnia, each two-ton bundle of bouncing pink biomass fidgets to the rhythms of his neighbors' snores. Brush up on wildlife at the island's reading room, located inside the lone outhouse. Back at your grassy camp, red fox peer into your tent, where on calm evenings you'll be serenaded by the wistful strumming sounds of contented walruses.

Marion, Montana

Hargrave Cattle &

Before barbed wire sewed up the last of the Western frontier, the Great Plains were wide boulevards for the seasonal movement of cattle. To sink your teeth into the red meat of a Wild West adventure, gallop over to the Hargrave Cattle & Guest Ranch, where punching, roping, and branding come with the territory. Ponderosa pines shoulder the dirt

Guest Ranch

lane that leads to the venerable log ranch and its lush meadow, fenced by sierra and brushed by the Thompson River. Driven by cowboys seeking greener pastures, distant herds out of a Remington painting kick a golden trail of swirling dust toward the rising sun. Returning to the ranch, the bovine cacophony is funneled inside corrals and shuffled into pens. At the dinner bell, leave your chaps by the door, wolf down homemade chili, and trade yarns with the wranglers. When Technicolor pastels tint the peaks, settle into your Rocky Mountain home on the range and listen to coyotes howling at the moon.

Everglades National Park, Florida

Sunday Bay
Chickee

An intimate encounter with the unique
ecosystem at the heart of the Everglades
requires some effort. Keen map-reading
skills and several hours of rowing by

canoe (earning calloused hands and sore behinds) are the minimum requirements for reaching this primitive accommodation in remote Sunday Bay. Gliding beneath bald cypress trees draped in Spanish moss and through a bewildering labyrinth of mangrove swamps, you reemerge into daylight among thick stands of sawgrass prairie, startling egrets into flight and rousing sunbathing turtles from their stumps. Here at last, hovering on stilts above alligator-choked waters, is the chickee, a roofed wooden platform based on traditional dwellings of the Seminole Indians who have made a peaceable life amid this harsh but hauntingly beautiful environment. As dusk approaches, crickets and cicadas weave a chorus of undulating crescendos. Evening dress code mandates a mesh-screened suit to minimize the effects of the Everglades' 46 or so varieties of thirsty mosquitoes.

Luxor

Managing to visually overpower even in
the neon playground that is Las Vegas, the
Luxor's soaring pyramid towers over the floor
of the Mojave like a desert mirage. Guarding
its entrance is a sphinx twice the size of the
Giza original. Just beyond, a stone-faced
bellboy leads visitors into the world's largest
lobby, under whose sloping roof nine
Boeing 747's can be handily stacked.

Diagonally ascend to a room fit for a pharaoh in the "inclinators," which manage to hew to their tracks at a 39-degree angle with surprising aplomb. A vertiginous peek from your balcony offers a vista of Mayan temples and an entire city skyline dwarfing a vast indoor district of theaters and shopping arcades. Snaking around the edge of it all is a heavily chlorinated Nile, where you can board an Egyptian barge and float past a simulated Abu Simbel and through an ancient valley of coffee shops and slot machines where the sun never shines or sets.

Mt. Washington, New Hampshire

Lakes of the
Clouds Hut

Just reaching the barely earthbound hut at the edge of Lakes of the Clouds is an adventure. It gets off to a bone-jarring start as you chug up a dizzily steep set of tracks on a toylike coal-fired cog railroad belching sparking embers. At the line's terminus, New England's ultimate pinnacle is buffeted by the most violent winds ever recorded on the surface of the earth. Cocoon yourself in layers before venturing onto the cairn-guided moonscape of the Appalachian Trail, which will likely descend through a meteorological battlefield of wind, thick fog, and driving rain or snow—signs warn that many unprepared climbers have died of overexposure here. On a rocky ridge overlooking infinity, a cedar-shingled cottage offers rustic bunks and all-you-can-eat meals. After a stroll around the glacial tarn to visit the planet's only patch of dwarf cinquefoil, snatch the top bunk to sleep on the highest bed in all the Northeast.

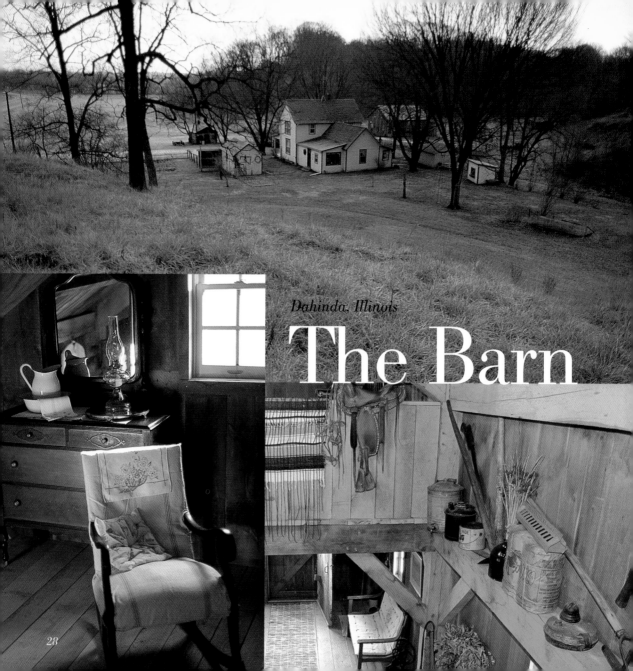

Dahinda, Illinois

The Barn

Driving through central Illinois's bucolic hinterlands, where the fabled Spoon River undulates through farmland striped with soybeans and embroidered with neatly stacked bales of hay, you stumble on a cluster of farm buildings at the edge of nowhere. Here a rusty red timber-frame barn, assembled with wood pegs from the remnants of less fortunate sheds, provides a serendipitous retreat for weary urbanites seeking down-on-the-farm peace. Lit by oil lamps, quilted sleeping quarters nestle in the open hayloft among hanging dried herbs and agrarian dioramas of vintage tools. Below the rafters is a full kitchen stuffed into the horse stall and a claw-foot tub for soaking in the oat-bin's bathroom. After a breakfast at the farmhouse, head out to the old stage-coach trail, crossed by deer and wild turkey, to hunt for flint tools and the meaning of life. As evening immerses the gully, enjoy the mournful crooning of distant freight trains bypassing your tranquil world.

JailHouse Inn

Arrest is no longer required for
incarceration in the former Fillmore

County Jail, now the JailHouse Inn.
This brick Italianate structure, near
the center of an agricultural village in
rolling Amish farmland, was built
in 1869 with only two cells—
apparently sufficient to contain the
entire county's criminal population. At
their arraignment, guests are sentenced
to negotiate a warren of Victorian-
flavored suites converted from the
courtroom and other public areas; but
hardened criminal minds will go
directly to the original cellblock. As
the bars clang shut behind you, rocking
chairs and quilted comforters ease the
burden of doing time in a correctional
facility whose bath temperature
is the only correction you might want
to make. You know you're in the
slammer when the spring-loaded toilet
seat snaps at your derriere, making
sure that the seat and the hygiene
standards stay up.

Lakeville, Pennsylvania

Caesars Cove Haven

Little did the tribes who once inhabited the Poconos know that their fertility ceremonies would be supplanted by the mating rituals being performed at the brood of kitschy honeymoon resorts these knobby hills have spawned. The ultimate fruition of a potent imagination is Caesars Cove Haven, at the edge of woodsy Lake Wallenpaupack, where horse-drawn buggies whisk you off into the land of love. Arriving at your windowless love den is like stumbling into an X-rated Disneyland where the fireworks are

muffled by heavily carpeted walls. The four-level suite features a round bed, a dry sauna, and a very wet heart-shaped pool just large enough for a frisky couple to cavort in. The climax of this private petting zoo is the patented seven-foot-tall champagne-glass whirlpool. Toast a new marriage while bobbing like cherries in a cocktail— an almost redundant aphrodisiac in a cup designed for an effervescent round of romance.

Boundary Waters Canoe Wilderness Area, Minnesota

Lake Bedew Yurts

Bursting with nervous canine energy, a yelping team of Alaskan huskies hurtles your sled at breakneck speeds across crystalline forest toward faraway Lake Bedew. Getting to the pair of round canvas yurts that squat along its banks depends on both the aerobic strength of these endurance-bred marathon mutts and your braking skills as you whoosh down brambled slopes and across frozen kettle ponds. Negotiating a hushed landscape where woodpeckers telegraph the weather report, pine martens scamper for seeds, and creaking evergreens bend under dollops of fresh snow, you reach the yurts, skylit oases of smoking warmth amid the frosted woodland. Shed those mukluks and recharge your depleted energy with a communal fondue simmering in a charcoal-seared Mongolian firepot. As daylight fades, wailing dogs answer the call of the wild, exchanging echoed messages with distant wolves. By the comforting crackle of a potbellied stove, snuggle into your bunk under a shimmering blanket of northern lights.

Hallam, Pennsylvania

Shoe House

Sticking out like a sore toe amid the rolling foothills of Pennsylvania's Alleghenies, the Shoe House is anything but a pedestrian home. An eccentric millionaire built it in the 1940s as an advertisement to promote his growing shoe-manufacturing empire, enshrining himself in the cement dwelling's stained-glass windows. Standing as an architectural footprint of Brobdingnagian proportions, this bed-and-breakfast is the consummate homage to footwear. Modeled after a high-topped work shoe, the house has a kitchen in the heel, two storybook bedrooms as well as a maid's room up a curvy turn of the ankle, and a living room that nicely fills out the toe. As if to ensure that the subtle point is not missed, the grounds feature a doghouse and a children's sandbox shaped like boots, while even the mail must conform to a postal shoe box. Tiptoeing back into the nursery-rhyme environment, slip into soulful dreams on Mother Goose themes.

Indianapolis, Indiana

Crowne

In the last century, when four train lines were vying to punch the public's tickets to Indianapolis, the notion of bunching them together under one roof was conceived, sparking the creation of union stations all across the country.

Plaza Union Station

In 1888, the city erected the majestic brick-and-granite Romanesque Revival terminal, with acres of stained glass dressing the walls and barrel-vaulted ceiling of the great hall. At the freight depot, you can now check into the Crowne Plaza, where an eager redcap, bypassing the more prosaic lodgings, makes sure your baggage gets all aboard a restored Pullman sleeper car from the 1920s. Wooden venetian blinds and antique buffalo-horn chairs re-create the ambiance of the golden age of steam within the cozy confines of your 200-ton suite. There's no need for an alarm clock—the Amtrak *Cardinal* comes flying across the adjacent tracks at 6:25 AM, bound for Chicago and points west.

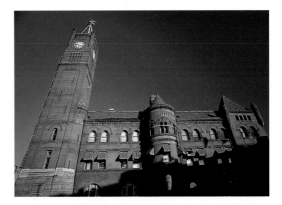

West Arlington, Vermont
The Inn at Covered Bridge Green

As a rich palette of deciduous color paints the Green Mountains, drive over the rattling planks of a covered bridge directly into a living Norman Rockwell canvas. At the edge of a postcard-perfect illustration of a New England village green, where the white-steepled church still fills for harvest suppers and the dusty grange welcomes farmers for square dancing, is the 200-year-old farmhouse where the artist honed his unique vignettes of small-town Americana. Today it is a charming inn, ringed by apple orchards that supply the pressed cider often served at breakfast. Out back is Rockwell's studio, warmed by a fire on snowy days, where a leisurely afternoon can be spent at the loveseat, puzzling over jigsaw versions of his paintings by the soaring picture windows. Scramble upstairs to your bedroom past the artist's beloved bicycle, proudly displayed on a wall, and his odd lightbulb-spoked wagonwheel hanging from the ceiling. In the place where artworks and props were once stashed, put your cares into storage and sketch a vivid dream.

Little Torch Key, Florida

Little Palm Island

Motor down the causeway that skips the Florida Keys to the former aquarium on Little Torch Key. After checking in, sail off as dolphins frolic and pelicans dive-bomb for brunch. Settle in at Little Palm Island, a Bali Hai–like paradise where bending palms reveal bungalows that open onto a sugar-white beach,

then laze on floats over waving fields of eelgrass or ride a pontoon-floated bike to observe brilliantly plumed roseate spoonbills on nearby islets. In the afternoon, let the hotel seaplane maroon you on a remote atoll with a picnic lunch and a snorkel. Back at your bungalow, shower in your hidden garden, then head toward the coral-crusted Great House. For the ultimate sybaritic dinner, silver settings and a sumptuous meal grace tables sunk into the pillowy-soft, torchlit sands beyond the patio. During dessert, diminutive Key deer cautiously approach to see about gourmet leftovers. Melt dreamily into a canopied bed, soothed by tree-frog lullabies.

Chesuncook, Maine

Chesuncook Lake House

The most useful tools for penetrating the Allagash wilderness are a canoe and a paddle. To reach the Chesuncook Lake House, some 20 miles from the nearest lumber-company road, follow the downstream currents on the West Branch of the Penobscot River. As raptors glide overhead, you'll spot moose rummaging through bankside fens and pass the streams where Thoreau once fished for philosophical ideas. Suddenly the birch-lined corridor opens to reveal immense stretches of pristine lake and, on its shore, the hamlet of Chesuncook, which consists of a church, an inn, some farmhouses, a permanent population of three or four people, and the haunting aura of generations of lumberjacks. Purchase some homemade root beer, then pick blueberries as you amble the flowered path to the Victorian inn, with its commanding view of Mt. Katahdin. After a hearty dinner, served near the cast-iron stove under pressed-tin ceilings, retire to the uninterrupted bedtime songs of the loons.

Windsong

Crowning one of the pastel ridges that
melt into perpetual mists in the Smokies,
some of the oldest mountains on earth,
is Windsong, a striking timbered inn
offering tasteful contemporary digs.
Surrounded by llama pastures, it is the
hub of myriad paths where these woolly
four-legged backpacks, toting up to
80 pounds of gear each, lead the way
up to crested vistas or down to brook-
etched dells. With discreet elimination
habits and padded two-toed feet that
won't scar trails, they are worthy
companions, spitting only occasionally
as they lope through the hemlock and
rhododendron groves of Pisgah National
Forest. At your sylvan picnic grounds,
chablis toasts preface chicken-and-
mushroom crepes amid a quirky
wilderness experience that adds a
whole new dimension to takeout food.
On optional sleepouts, soak up the
warmth of a campfire social circle,
then join in the chorus of off-key llama
tunes hummed nonchalantly until the
wee hours.

Nothing's ordinary at Randall's Ordinary,
a 1685 farmhouse whose surname derives
from the taverns of an earlier era.

North Stonington, Connecticut
Randall's
Ordinary

The taproom does dispense Colonial libations, but the real intoxication beneath the hand-hewn beams emanates from the inn's central fireplace, a smoky epicurean theater around which hearth-side cooking is performed thrice daily. Granite charred by three centuries of smoldering oak and hickory sets the scene for costumed servers straight out of *Tom Jones*, who tend the glowing coals and check mulligatawny stews percolating in hanging iron caldrons. A harpist spins melodies as roast venison is yanked from clouds of steam and Nantucket scallops sizzle over huge flame-licked skillets, prepared according to recipes gleaned from period cookbooks. Still under the spell of this gastronomic time warp, retire upstairs to your own private fire and curtained four-poster. By the dawn's early light, the fragrant wakeup call of coriander-ginger bread incubating in beehive ovens will waft through the cracks in your creaky floorboards.

Out 'n' About

Tucked into the shady fringe of a primeval grove, four scattered treehouses stand sentry in Oregon's majestic Siskiyou range. When the wind blows, these arboreal cradles will rock among budding tendrils of white oak. The veranda goes way out on a limb; from there you can survey a distant kingdom of serrated ridge tops thick with forest. Hungry blue jays patrol the borders of the next-door cedar as ruby-throated hummingbirds flit hyperactively around branches bearded with lichen. Step through a frieze-like door of chiseled wood, across a polished floor laid with a comfy futon, to the windows, you'll spot a pair of seemingly ramshackle habitats linked by a hanging bridge and reached by a ladder and a secret trap door. Play Tarzan, swinging back to the ground floor by a dangling rope, then head out to explore, discovering yet another fairy-tale hostelry clinging to the canopy like a Swiss Family Robinson hallucination. In the cirrus-streaked moonlight, doze in your treetop nest to a nocturne for hooting owls and whispering leaves.

Treehouse Resort

Franklin, West Virginia
McCoy's Mill

In the 19th century, water mills built to harness nature's gravitational force sprang up all across America's growing frontier settlements. In the Monongahela range, where gurgling streams and thundering waterfalls scratch through craggy highlands, McCoy's Mill still operates, but as a rustic bed-and-breakfast. In a remote hollow carved by Thorn Creek as it spills into the headwaters of the Potomac, the site is the state's oldest landmark. Tough buhrstone wheels once used to grind the yields of neighboring cornfields lie by the entrance to the four-story post-and-beam mill house. After a breakfast of French-toast casserole and savory apple butter, while away the hours trout fishing or just creaking in the porch's hickory rockers. Later, listen to some Appalachian fiddle and banjo tunes at a nearby tavern, then return to your hand-carved cannonball bed for a solid snooze to the cascading white noise of the turbine's endlessly twirling waterwheel.

San Luis Obispo, California

Madonna Inn

The Madonna Inn is the ultimate expression of a motel gone berserk. A wildly spun confection of lacy wooden furbelows and commanding 200-ton boulders, the lodging was painstakingly crafted with the whimsical imagination and leftover materials of a contractor who helped build the adjacent Pacific Coast Highway. From postcard racks in the lobby, pick one of the loopy stage-set rooms in this rambling residential theme park where guests hatcheck reality for a night in Wonderland. Beneath a winding, hand-carved balustrade from nearby Hearst Castle, the main dining room is a shocking pink candy box of leatherette booths, etched glass, and a copper-wired tree chandelier that would have made Liberace blush. Women shyly peek into the public men's room, which hides giant clamshell sinks and inviting urinals where cascading waterfalls plummet rocky cliffs. Hail a surrey back to your room, with its water-wheel cuckoo clock; shower in a cave; or hit the sack in a buckboard wagon.

Memphis, Tennessee

Peabody Hotel

Wildlife viewing may seem unlikely in a downtown webbed by trolley lines, barbecue joints, and blues clubs. Nevertheless, Memphis's Peabody Hotel, a bastion of elegance renowned throughout the Mississippi Delta, is a magnet for birdwatchers. Each morning they arrive, awaiting their first sighting as they cluster under the chandeliers suspended from the lobby's stained-glass ceiling. Moments before the clock strikes eleven, a red carpet is unrolled, Sousa's "King Cotton March" strikes up, and the elevator doors open. As Southern whiskeys are suddenly abandoned at the smoky bar, necks strain, camera flashes ignite, and four mallard hens and a drake emerge—escorted on their waddling trek down the carpet by a straight-faced, uniformed duckmaster—to enjoy an afternoon splashing among tinkling cherubs in the travertine fountain. The ceremony reverses at 5 PM, when the avian shepherd gets all his ducks in a row and marches them back to their penthouse high above both the skyline and 12 floors of royal chambers designed for human occupation.

Akron, Ohio

Inn at Quaker Square

As you roll across the vast, plaid wheat fields of the Midwest, the next town on the flour-white horizon is often announced by the silhouettes of its grain elevators—storage towers that are the commercial heart of the nation's breadbasket. If you're really feeling your oats and want to sleep in one, pull off the interstate and into downtown Akron, where the Inn at Quaker Square commands attention with its thirty-six concrete turn-of-the-century silos. Along with the adjoining brick-and-timber Quaker Oats factory mill, they have been imaginatively redesigned into a hotel complex where the original shafts and ducts are interspersed with a sprinkling of shops, markets and restaurants (that serve oatmeal). Out back, climb the freight locomotives that once helped deliver the puffed grains shot from guns to breakfast tables around the nation. Returning to the hotel's perfectly circular rooms, fall asleep in your very own cereal bowl.

Fall River, Massachusetts

U.S.S. Massachusetts

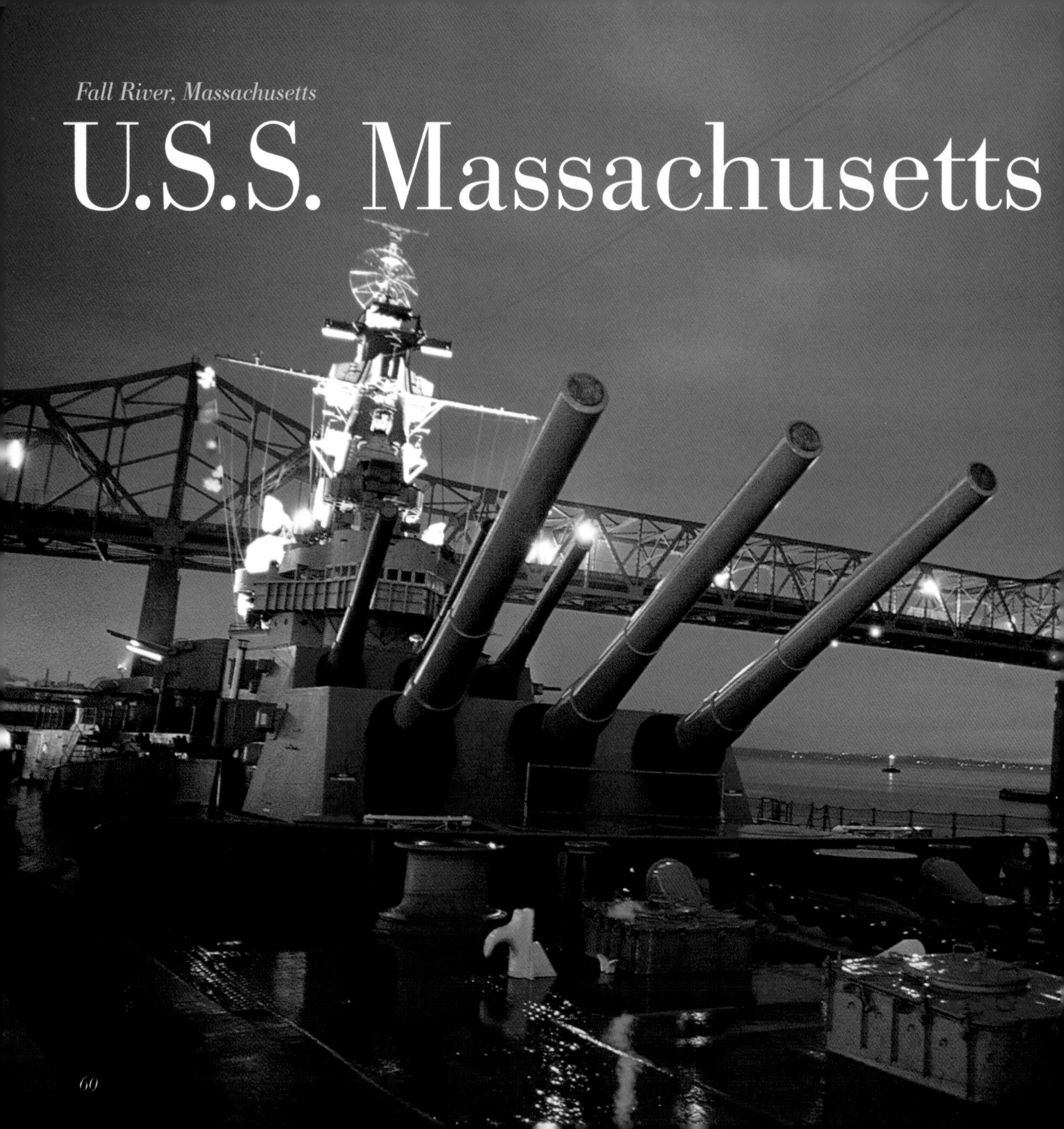

March up the gangway to this decommissioned battleship standing sentry near an entrance to Mt. Hope Bay. Stow your gear, then climb inside the gun turrets, rotate the antiaircraft weaponry, and investigate the massive barrels, which are capable of ejecting a ballistic cargo as heavy as a Volkswagen for a distance of over 25 miles. Chow down in the Officer's Wardroom, do your time on KP duty, then you're again free to wander the decks of this nine-story leviathan that sprawls over the length of two football fields. Squeeze through skinny corridors crowded with torpedoes past metallic cubbyholes stitched together by intimidating hatches, then climb to the bridge for a lookout over the seaport. Hours may be spent examining miles of museum exhibits depicting the action this highly decorated ship saw in World War II. After taps, at 2300 hours, surrender consciousness to the narrow canvas bunks suspended by chains in the bowels of the ship.

Pollywogg Hollër

At the start of a mossy path, grab the kerosene lamp and wheelbarrow your luggage across trestled board-walks, past organic vegetable beds, and through a lush grove's enchanting sculpture garden. As you enter the magical whimsy of Pollywogg Hollër, the sibilant rush of a creekside falls announces a wonderfully weird handcrafted paradise seemingly inhabited by a

hibernating troupe of hobbits. Cresting a knoll is the main building of this solar-powered, Great Camp-style ecolodge, where later the glow of candles will frame a gourmet meal conjured with culinary sorcery on the wood-burning stove or in the outdoor adobe kiln. For now, your private cottage, the honeymoon loft, awaits. Pass under the awning, braced by fanciful tree-trunk ornamentation radiant under the glow of a lantern-lit stained-glass chandelier. Inside is an intimate pine-fired sauna whose fragrant vapors warm the separate sleeping quarters just above it. After dinner, come back to soak up the steamy heat, shower beneath a pulley-hoisted barrel filled with spring water, then, feeling like a troll, clamber up teeny footholds to the attic and its cloud-soft mattress, where reality's tensions will soon evaporate.

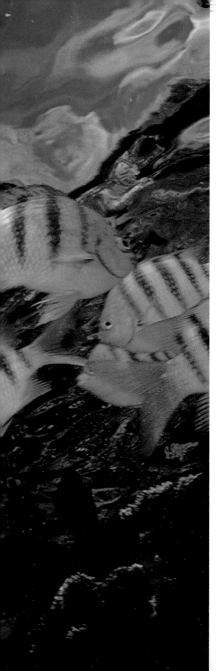

Key Largo, Florida

Jules Undersea Lodge

Strap on scuba gear and follow a trail of opalescent bubbles down to your evening's accommodations, in a former scientific habitat 30 feet below the surface of a coral lagoon. As you wind through billowing curtains of parrotfish, the barnacled hulk on the ocean floor looms ever larger. Once safely in the lobby, you may kick off your flippers and breathe again without tanks. Soon your watertight luggage is delivered by an aquatic bellman. He will return later to double as microwaving chef in this reverse aquarium, where curious nurse sharks observe through the porthole as the human residents are fed daily. After a lobster dinner, take a hookah-powered twilight stroll across a darkening cove illuminated by phosphorescent plankton, followed by a suboceanic viewing of *20,000 Leagues Under the Sea* played on the VCR. As the credits roll, sink into deep sleep to the sound-track of the burbling life-support system.

Oak Park, Illinois
Cheney House

Streaming to Oak Park to pay their respects
to a great visionary, knowledgeable pilgrims
gape in mystical communion with the
numerous buildings Frank Lloyd Wright
designed for this quiet Chicago suburb. It is
far more exciting, though, to actually inhabit
one of his American masterpieces. At the
Cheney House, now a bed-and-breakfast, the
geometric simplicity of Wright's earth-hugging
prairie style is striking. Brilliant legerdemain
creates a theatrical sense of free-flowing space
with peaked ceilings that shift dramatically in
height. In this residential jewel box, iridescent
art glass windows change hues as the sinking
sun fingers Wright-designed furniture, china,
and original lamp fixtures poised to set the
place aglow at dusk. The architect built the
house in 1903 for a lover and returned many
times, adding detail to both the woodwork
and his scandalous affair. In the first-known
platform bed, you too can now awaken to the
pitter-patter from his trademark leaky roof.

The austerely beautiful Shaker Village of Pleasant Hill offers a glimpse into the devout community that thrived here among the bluegrass meadows cut by limestone palisades. The meeting house was once the scene of frenzied dances to haunting a cappella melodies, the peculiar form of worship that gave the sect its name. Across the way, a former family dwelling offers simple rooms for overnight visitors. Inside are handwoven rugs, as well as the famed Shaker furniture and pegboards. Out back, an herb garden yields prizewinning seeds for sale and sauces for the candlelit dining room, where bonneted servers dish up well-seasoned corn pudding and heavenly jam cakes. In village workshops, craftsmen weave a tapestry of hard work and creative virtuosity into an enduring legacy. Shortly, when the last of the Shakers' elderly members depart for another world, the faith will disappear—not surprising, for when a religion's principal tenet is complete abstinence, it's bound to run out of genetic gas sooner or later.

Harrodsburg, Kentucky

Shaker Village of

Pleasant Hill

Gem Peak Lookout Tower

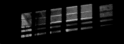

Steady nerves compete with bumpy dirt roads as you maneuver your four-wheel-drive on a cliff-hanging ride toward the rooftop of Montana. An eagle's swoop from the Continental Divide, atop 6,000-foot Gem Peak, a glass-and-wood matchbox teeters on stilts above stunted pines and golden larches. Once part of an extensive system of U.S. Forest Service fire lookouts, made obsolete by modern aircraft surveillance, it is now a breathtaking platform for aerial sleepovers. After a rigorous climb, tread the narrow catwalk and enter a room boasting little more than a woodstove, a food cupboard, basic bedding, candles for light, and a vintage firefinder. What this spartan solarium encased in 112 windowpanes offers instead is a dizzying, wraparound view of mountainous silhouettes and roaming elk set against cerulean skies that shift into the screaming oranges of sunset. Weather in big-sky country changes rapidly, and just as easily those windows can be filled with electrical pitchforks dancing from scudding nimbus clouds. As the insistent wind of evening attempts to wrestle the glass from its frames, lie back and wait for the storm to pass, then nap in your swaying planetarium under a diamond-studded ceiling.

Waikoloa Village

The last resort for those convinced they've seen everything, the Waikoloa Village drapes an entire mile of the Kohala coast, on the sun-drenched lee side of Hawaii's volcanic Big Island. The complex straddles a bed of lava etched with ancient petroglyphs. To reach your own bed, hop a monorail, or travel by yacht along a canal that meanders through forests of bamboo and towering monkeypods, past waterfall-slapped pools strung together by streams where cranes and flamingos crowd the banks. At your tropical abode, a secluded lanai drips with fragrant bougainvillea and unveils a wide-screen Polynesian fantasyland. Down by the beach-rimmed saltwater lagoon, swim with a pod of bottle-nosed dolphins who, with their clicks and whistles, seem to express enjoyment in shaking flippers with their human playmates. Gazing into the curious eyes and souls of another species, you realize you may never really see everything after all.

DIRECTORY

ALASKA

Walrus Islands State Game Sanctuary
Walrus Camps
Box 1030
Dillingham, AK 99576
tel. 907/842-2334
fax 907/842-5514

$50 per person for 5-day permit; water available. Request permit when reserving. No credit cards. Open May 1–Aug. 15. Don's Round Island Charters, Box 68, Togiak, AK 99678, tel. 907/493-5127.

ARIZONA/UTAH

Lake Powell Houseboats
Lake Powell Resort & Marinas
Box 56909
Phoenix, AZ 85079
tel. 602/278-8888 or 800/528-6154
fax 602/331-5294

$723–$2,276 for 3–7 nights. Boats depart from Wahweap Lodge & Marina, Box 1597, Page, AZ 86040, tel. 520/645-2433, fax 520/645-5175, and from three more remote Utah marinas. AE, D, DC, MC, V.

CALIFORNIA

Madonna Inn
100 Madonna Rd.
San Luis Obispo, CA 93405
tel. 805/543-3000 or 800/543-9666
fax 805/543-1800
www.madonnainn.com

109 rooms and suites. $77–$210. MC, V.

CONNECTICUT

Randall's Ordinary
Rte. 2, Box 243
North Stonington, CT 06359
tel. 860/599-4540
fax 860/599-3308

3 rooms in main house, 2 in barn. $55–$195 Sun.–Thurs., $115–$195 Fri.–Sat.; includes Continental breakfast. AE, MC, V.

FLORIDA

Jules Undersea Lodge
51 Shore Land Dr.
Key Largo, FL 33037
tel. 305/451-2353
fax 305/451-4789

2 bedrooms, common room, and bath. 1 bedroom: $195 per person (5 PM–9 AM) with light dinner and breakfast, $295 per person with unlimited diving and gourmet dinner and breakfast. Exclusive use: $1,000 for 2 with unlimited diving, gourmet dinner and breakfast, and more. AE, D, MC, V. Guests must scuba-dive to lodge; those not certified can take a 3-hour class and dive with the instructor.

Little Palm Island
28500 Overseas Hwy.
Little Torch Key, FL 33042
tel. 305/872-2524 or 800/343-8567
fax 305/872-4843

28 suites in 14 thatched cottages, 1 poolside suite, and 1 houseboat suite. $330–$645. No children under 12. AE, D, DC, MC, V. Boat or seaplane to island by arrangement.

Sunday Bay Chickee
Gulf Coast Visitors Center
Box 120
Everglades City, FL 34139
tel. 941/695-3311
fax 941/695-3621

10- by 12-foot double chickee with docking facilities. A backcountry camping permit is required and can be obtained in person up to 24 hours in advance at the Flamingo Visitor Center. Essential packing list: a nautical chart (available at local marinas or from the Florida Parks and Monuments Association, tel. 305/247-1216), a compass, a freestanding tent with netting, basic gear, and water and food. For more information, contact Everglades National Park, 40001 State Rd. 9336, Homestead, FL 33034-6733, tel. 305/242-7700, fax 305/242-7728. North American Canoe Tours, tel. 941/695-4666 (canoes $20 first day, $18 each consecutive day; kayaks $35–$45 daily) offers complete outfitting and guided overnight canoe trips.

HAWAII

Hilton Waikoloa Village
425 Waikoloa Beach Dr.
Kamuela, HI 96743
tel. 808/885-1234
fax 808/885-2900

1,238 rooms. $280–$340. AE, D, DC, MC, V.

The Barn
Box 92
Dahinda, IL 61428
tel. 309/639-4408
fax 309/639-4408

Sleeps seven. Single $60, double $70,
$35 per extra person over two; includes
Continental breakfast (full breakfast
available). No credit cards.

Cheney House
520 N. East Ave.
Oak Park, IL 60302
tel. 708/524-2067
fax 312/236-0860

Double room $100; 2-bedroom master
suite with king-size bed, living room,
whirlpool, and fireplace $155;
includes Continental breakfast. MC, V.

Crowne Plaza Union Station
123 W. Louisiana St.
Indianapolis, IN 46225
tel. 317/631-2221
fax 317/236-7474

26 Pullman train-car rooms. $165–$200.
AE, D, DC, MC, V.

Shaker Village of Pleasant Hill
3501 Lexington Rd.
Harrodsburg, KY 40330
tel. 606/734-5411
fax 606/734-5411

81 rooms. $50–$100. MC, V.

Delta Queen
Robin St. Wharf
1380 Port of New Orleans Pl.
New Orleans, LA 70130-1890
tel. 800/543-1949
fax 504/585-0630

87 staterooms. 3 nights $163 per person
per night (double occupancy) and up,
3–14 nights $490–$1,840; includes
4 meals a day and entertainment. AE,
DC, MC, V.

Chesuncook Lake House
Rte. 76, Box 656
Greenville, ME 04441
tel. 207/745-5330
(phone connection is via radiophone)

Lake house: 4 double rooms, $85 per
person; includes meals and transportation.
3 cottages (2–3 rooms): $68 per person
with meals and some transportation,
$35 without meals (kitchen available).
No credit cards. Open May–late fall.
Transportation by boat, plane, or
canoe by arrangement.

Keeper's House
Box 26
Isle au Haut, ME 04645
tel. 207/367-2261

4 rooms in keeper's house, 2 rooms
in separate cottages. 1 person in room,
$175; 2 in room, $250; 3 in room,
$300; includes 3 meals, box lunches
for day hikes, use of inn's bikes.
No credit cards. Open May–Oct.
Mailboats from the Isle au Haut
Company (tel. 207/367-5193) take
passengers from Stonington to the
island Monday–Saturday except post
office holidays ($5–$10 per person).
Half of the island belongs to Acadia
National Park, which has many
hiking trails.

U.S.S. *Massachusetts*
Battle Cove
Fall River, MA 02721
tel. 508/678-1100 or 800/533-3194
fax 508/674-5597

Accommodates up to 500 in bunks.
$33 per person; includes 3 meals in
mess hall. MC, V.

Banadad Yurts
Boundary Country Trekking
590 Gunflint Trail
Grand Marais, MN 55604
tel. 218/388-4487 or 800/322-8327
fax 218/388-4487
bct@boreal.org
www.boreal.org/adventures

$120 per person per night; includes
all meals and shuttle service for gear
and your car. Guests either ski or
dogsled to the yurt from a cabin or
lodge at the end of the trail. Yurt-to-
yurt and other packages available.
MC, V. Open mid-Dec–Apr.

JailHouse Inn
Box 422
109 Houston St.
Preston, MN 55965
tel. 507/765-2181
fax 507/765-2558

12 rooms. $40–$149; includes
Continental breakfast. DC, MC, V.

Gem Peak Lookout Tower
Cabinet Ranger District
2693 Hwy. 200
Trout Creek, MT 59874
tel. 406/827-3533
fax 406/827-3203

$25 for 4 (only 1 single bed provided).
All camping gear, food, and water
must be carried in. A permit is
required and may be obtained in
person or by mail from the Ranger
District. (Other towers are also
available.) No credit cards. Open
mid-June–Oct.

Hargrave Cattle & Guest Ranch
300 Thompson River Rd.
Marion, MT 59925
tel. 406/858-2284 or 800/933-0696
fax 406/858-2284

3 cabins for families and groups,
couples and singles in the headquarters.
Full board $1,050 per person per
week May–mid-Oct., $100 per person
per day mid-Oct.–Apr.; includes 3
meals and most recreational activities.
Bed-and-breakfast $60 single, $80
double; lunch or dinner $20 extra per
person. MC, V.

Luxor
3900 Las Vegas Blvd.
Las Vegas, NV 89119
tel. 702/262-4000 or 800/288-1000
fax 702/262-4452

4,496 rooms. $59–$259. AE, D, DC,
MC, V.

Lakes of the Clouds Hut
Appalachian Mountain Club
Rte. 16, Box 298
Gorham, NH 03581
tel. 603/466-2727
fax 603/466-3871

Accommodates 90 guests in 8 bunk-
rooms sleeping 6, 8, 12, or 15. Adults
$37–$62; includes breakfast and dinner.
Hike in, take the Mt. Washington cog
railroad (tel. 603/846-5404), or use the
road on the other side of the mountain.
MC, V. Open June–mid-Sept. (7 other
huts available, some open all year).

Mohonk Mountain House
Lake Mohonk
New Paltz, NY 12561
tel. 914/255-1000 or 800/772-6646
fax 914/256-2161

273 rooms. $109–$475; includes
3 meals, afternoon tea, and most
recreational activities. AE, D,
DC, MC, V.

Pollywogg Hollër
Belmont, NY 14813
tel. 716/268-5819
fax 716/268-5819

Main lodge with loft and bedchamber,
and a sauna guest house. $49–$74 per
person double occupancy. AE, V.

Windsong
120 Ferguson Ridge
Clyde, NC 28721
tel. 704/627-6111
fax 704/627-8080

5 rooms in lodge, $100–$115;
includes full breakfast. Pond House
Suite: 2 bedrooms, living/dining area
with wood-burning stove, bath with
tub for two, kitchen, and deck,
$140–$160; includes Continental
breakfast. D, MC, V. Llama treks
(124 Ferguson Ridge, Clyde, NC
28721, tel. 704/627-6986): day trek
$60 per person, dinner trek $35, and
overnight and 3-day treks $100.

Inn at Quaker Square
135 S. Broadway
Akron, OH 44308
tel. 330/253-5970
fax 330/253-2574

196 rooms. $90–$150. AE, D, DC,
MC, V.

Out 'n' About Treehouse Resort
300 Page Creek Rd.
Cave Junction, OR 97523
tel. 541/592-2208 or 800/200-5484
fax 541/592-4143

Family complex: $75 per night for up
to 4 people. Deluxe treehouse: $65 per
night for up to 3 people. Tree-room
clubhouse suite with kitchenette and
bath: $125 per night for up to 6 people.
All prices include Continental breakfast
and "tree shirt." No credit cards.

Caesars Cove Haven
Rte. 590, Box 40
Lakeville, PA 18438
tel. 717/226-4506 or 800/233-4141
fax 717/226-4697

36 Cleopatra suites with champagne-
glass whirlpool baths. $380. Includes
full breakfast, dinner, and use of all
facilities. AE, MC, V. (Cleopatra suites
also available at other Caesars Pocono
properties.)

Shoe House
197 Shoe House La.
York, PA 17402
tel. 717/755-1296

3 rooms, 2 baths, living room, and
kitchen. B&B option available. $75–$100.
No credit cards.

Peabody Hotel
149 Union Ave.
Memphis, TN 38103
tel. 901/529-4000 or 800/732-2639
fax 901/529-3600

468 rooms. Rooms $130–$240, suites
$250–$1,345. AE, DC, MC, V.

The Inn at Covered Bridge Green
R.D. 1, Box 3550
Arlington, VT 05250
tel. 802/375-9489
fax 802/375-1208

Loft in studio: $140–$180 per night
for 2. 5 rooms in inn: $110–$140;
includes full breakfast. AE (surcharge).

McCoy's Mill
Thorn Creek Rd.
Box 610
Franklin, WV 26807
tel. 304/358-7893.

3 rooms. $50 single, $60 double.
Includes full country breakfast. Kitchen;
$30 charge for cooking. MC, V.